你好

Nǐ Hǎo

②

Student Workbook

Elementary Level

by

Shumang Fredlein ● Paul Fredlein

ChinaSoft

Nǐ Hǎo 2 – Student Workbook – Elementary Level
First Published 1993; reprinted 1994, 1995, 1997, 1999
New edition 2002; reprinted 2004, 2006

ChinaSoft Pty Ltd   ABN: 61 083 458 459
P.O. Box 845, Toowong, Brisbane, Qld 4066, AUSTRALIA
Telephone (61-7) 3371-7436
Facsimile (61-7) 3371-6711
www.chinasoft.com.au

Written by Shumang Fredlein（林淑满）& Paul Fredlein
Illustrated by Zhengdong Su（苏正东）& Xiaolin Xue（薛曉林）
Edited by Sitong Jan（詹絲桐）
Typeset by ChinaSoft on Apple Macintosh

Printed in Australia by Watson Ferguson & Company, Brisbane

Textbook, audio CDs, audio cassettes and Games software also available.

ISBN 1 876739 13 4

Foreword

The *Ni Hao 2 Student Workbook* is a learning activity book based on the content introduced in the *Ni Hao 2 Textbook - Chinese Language Course, Elementary Level*. This workbook contains a variety of activities that provide opportunities for students to practise the four communication skills - listening, speaking, reading and writing. Activities can be adapted to suit students' needs and abilities, e.g. the listening exercises can be used for speaking; the reading and writing exercises can also be used for listening and speaking.

The listening exercises for each lesson are included in the Teacher's Handbook and recorded on audio cassettes/CDs. The teacher may play the cassette to the class, or alternatively, read out the passages from the Teacher's Handbook. Answers to all the questions in this book are included in the Teacher's Handbook.

Chinese characters are used in conjunction with Pinyin to reinforce reading and writing skills. Students are not required to write exclusively in characters, but are encouraged to use a combination of Pinyin and characters. The Textbook lists characters students should learn to write. These characters are also included in the *Writing Exercise* section of this book. Students should always write characters in the correct stroke order and in good proportion. This provides the foundation for beautiful handwriting which is always appreciated by Chinese.

Contents

dì yī kè　wǒ de shēngrì
第 一 课　我 的 生 日

A　Listen to the statements and choose the correct answers.

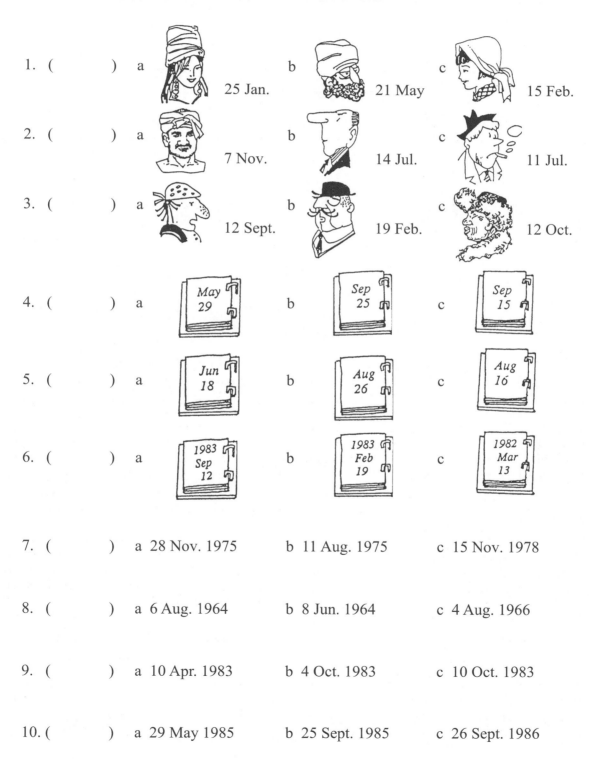

1. (　　) a　25 Jan.　b　21 May　c　15 Feb.

2. (　　) a　7 Nov.　b　14 Jul.　c　11 Jul.

3. (　　) a　12 Sept.　b　19 Feb.　c　12 Oct.

4. (　　) a　May 29　b　Sep 25　c　Sep 15

5. (　　) a　Jun 18　b　Aug 26　c　Aug 16

6. (　　) a　1983 Sep 12　b　1983 Feb 19　c　1982 Mar 13

7. (　　) a 28 Nov. 1975　b 11 Aug. 1975　c 15 Nov. 1978

8. (　　) a 6 Aug. 1964　b 8 Jun. 1964　c 4 Aug. 1966

9. (　　) a 10 Apr. 1983　b 4 Oct. 1983　c 10 Oct. 1983

10. (　　) a 29 May 1985　b 25 Sept. 1985　c 26 Sept. 1986

二

B You and your Chinese friend have decided to play tennis every Tuesday during the summer season. Use the calendar below and write these dates in Chinese to remind your friend.

_____   _____   _____

_____   _____   _____

_____   _____   _____

_____   _____   _____

_____   _____   _____

January
星期日　星期一　星期二　星期三　星期四　星期五　星期六

February
星期日　星期一　星期二　星期三　星期四　星期五　星期六

March
星期日　星期一　星期二　星期三　星期四　星期五　星期六

April
星期日　星期一　星期二　星期三　星期四　星期五　星期六

May
星期日　星期一　星期二　星期三　星期四　星期五　星期六

June
星期日　星期一　星期二　星期三　星期四　星期五　星期六

July
星期日　星期一　星期二　星期三　星期四　星期五　星期六

August
星期日　星期一　星期二　星期三　星期四　星期五　星期六

September
星期日　星期一　星期二　星期三　星期四　星期五　星期六

October
星期日　星期一　星期二　星期三　星期四　星期五　星期六

November
星期日　星期一　星期二　星期三　星期四　星期五　星期六

December
星期日　星期一　星期二　星期三　星期四　星期五　星期六

C You have several appointments on the following dates. Use the calendar on the previous page and write, in English, the days of the week on which they fall.

一月十八日 _____   二月二十五日 _____

三月十四日 _____   七月二十一日 _____

九月二十日 _____   五月二十八日 _____

十二月九日 _____   十一月三十日 _____

D Here are some famous Chinese. Write their dates of birth in Chinese.

1. Sūn Yìxiān
   孙逸仙 12 Nov. 1866 _____

2. Jiǎng Jièshí
   蒋介石 31 Oct. 1887 _____

3. Máo Zédōng
   毛泽东 26 Dec. 1893 _____

4. Zhōu Ēnlái
   周恩来 5 Mar. 1898 _____

5. Dèng Xiǎopíng
   邓小平 22 Aug. 1904 _____

E You are conducting a survey to find out your friends' dates of birth. Write the questions you need for your survey. Check your questions and conduct your survey to complete the table. Report your results to the class after your survey.

Q 1: To find out the year:

_____

Q 2: To find out the date:

_____

or

_____

Name	Date of Birth	Name	Date of Birth
(yourself)			

Your findings:

1. What is the percentage of people who were born in the same year as you?

2. What is the percentage of people who were born in the same month as you?

F　Answer the following questions according to the information given. Use complete sentences with as many characters as possible.

1. 今天是几月几号？星期几？

_____

2. 今天是一九九三年五月十二日，星期三。明天呢？

_____

3. 今天是不是八月二十六号？

_____

4. 今天是十一月十二号，对不对？

_____

5. 老师，我们明天去钓鱼，可以吗？
   <small>diàoyú</small>

_____

6. 我们明天去打乒乓球，好吗？
   <small>pīngpāngqiú</small>

_____

7. 你的生日是什么时候？
   <small>shíhou</small>

_____

G What should you say in Chinese in the following situations? Use complete sentences with as many characters as possible.

1. To wish your friend happy birthday.

_____

2. To find out today's date.

_____

3. To find out what day of the week today is.

_____

4. To ask permission from your teacher to go to the toilet (厕所).
^{cèsuǒ}

_____

5. To tell someone that Ben and Don are twins.

_____

6. To say that you are going swimming with John tomorrow.

_____

7. To find out someone's birthday.

_____

8. To say that you thought it was Friday today.

_____

H Read the following paragraph about 林国明 and 李亚, then answer the questions.

_{Lín}　　　_{Lǐ}　　　_{tóngbān}　　　　　　　　　　_{qiántiān}　　　　　　_{Lín}
林国明和李亚是同班同学，也是好朋友。前天是四月十九日，林国明

_{Lǐ}　_{yóuyǒng}　　　　　　　　_{tī}　_{zúqiú}　　　　　　　　_{wǎngqiú}
和李亚去游泳。昨天他们去踢足球，今天他们去打网球。明天林国明想去

_{diàoyú}
钓鱼，李亚说："不行，明天是星期一，我们要上

学。"林国明说："明天是我的生日，我爸爸

说我可以不去上学。"李亚说："那么，你明天和

_{diàoyú}
你爸爸去钓鱼吧！"

1. What day is it today and what is the date?

2. Who is 李亚? What have 李亚 and 林国明 been doing?

3. When is 林国明 's birthday?

4. What is he likely to do on his birthday? Give reasons for your answer.

八

I Listen to the conversation between 王美怡 Wáng Měiyí and 李大中 Lǐ Dàzhōng then answer the following questions.

1. What is special about today?

2. What did 李大中 Lǐ Dàzhōng wish 王美怡 Wáng Měiyí and why?

3. When is 王美怡 Wáng Měiyí's birthday?

4. What is the date today?

In the box below, paste the copy of the conversation given to you by your teacher to further check your understanding. Use this copy to hold a conversation with your partner.

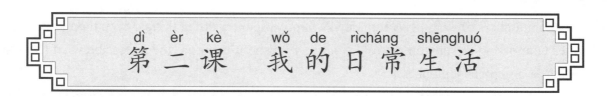

A Listen to the statements and choose the correct answers.

1. (　　　) a　　　　　　b　　　　　　c

2. (　　　) a　　　　　　b　　　　　　c

3. (　　　) a　　　　　　b　　　　　　c

4. (　　　) a　　　　　　b　　　　　　c

5. (　　　) a　　　　　　b　　　　　　c

6. (　　　) a　　　　　　b　　　　　　c

7. (　　　) a　　　　　　b　　　　　　c

8. (　　　) a　　　　　　b　　　　　　c

9. (　　　) a　　　　　　b　　　　　　c

10. (　　　) a　　　　　　b　　　　　　c

B All the members of 王美怡 Wáng Měiyí's family are busy doing things, even their pets. Draw lines connecting the person/pet to the activity he/she/it is doing; then describe what they are doing in complete sentences.

1. 美怡 (Měiyí)　　放风筝 (fàng fēngzhēng)　　_____

2. 爸爸　　下棋 (xiàqí)　　_____

3. 妈妈　　吃东西 (dōngxi)　　_____

4. 哥哥　　做功课 (gōngkè)　　_____

5. 姐姐　　看小人儿书 (xiǎorénrshū)　　_____

6. 妹妹　　睡觉 (shuìjiào)　　_____

7. 弟弟　　喝茶 (chá)　　_____

8. 小猫　　跳舞 (tiàowǔ)　　_____

9. 小狗　　看书　　_____

10. 小鸟　　听音乐 (tīng yīnyuè)　　_____

C Listen to the time stated on the tape and draw a clock face with the correct time. You can also use this to tell your class the time after you complete the drawing.

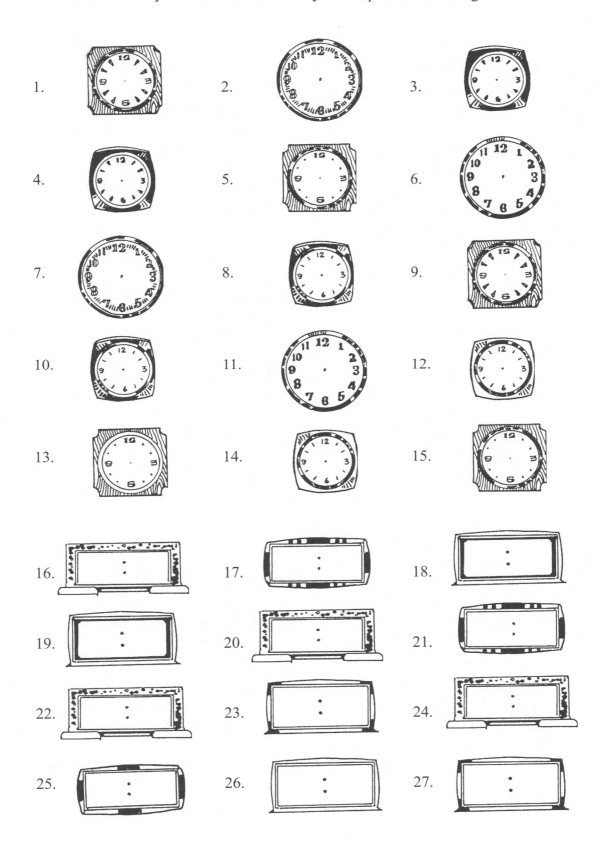

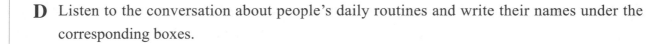

十二

D Listen to the conversation about people's daily routines and write their names under the corresponding boxes.

1.
```
get up - 7:00 a.m.
breakfast - 7:45 a.m.
go to school - 8:00 a.m.
lunch - 12:45 p.m.
finish school - 3:15 p.m.
football - 4:00 p.m.
dinner - 7:00 p.m.
homework - 8:00 p.m.
sleep - 10:00 p.m.
```

_____

2.
```
get up - 6:30 a.m.
breakfast - 7:00 a.m.
go to school - 7:30 a.m.
lunch - 12:30 p.m.
finish school - 3:00 p.m.
dinner - 6:30 p.m.
watch TV - 7:00 p.m.
homework - 8:00 p.m.
sleep - 9:30 pm.
```

_____

3.
```
get up - 7:30 a.m.
breakfast - 8:00 a.m.
go to school - 8:20 a.m.
lunch - 12:45 p.m.
finish school - 3:15 p.m.
swimming - 5:00 p.m.
dinner - 7:30 p.m.
homework - 9:00 p.m.
sleep - 10:30 p.m.
```

_____

4.
```
get up - 5:30 a.m.
swimming - 6:00 a.m.
breakfast - 7:00 a.m.
go to school - 7:30 a.m.
lunch - 12:30 p.m.
finish school - 3:00 p.m.
dinner - 6:30 p.m.
homework - 7:30 p.m.
sleep - 9:00 p.m.
```

_____

5.
```
get up - 5:30 a.m.
running - 6:00 a.m.
breakfast - 7:30 a.m.
go to school - 8:00 a.m.
lunch - 12:45 p.m.
finish school - 3:00 p.m.
dinner - 7:00 p.m.
homework - 8:00 p.m.
sleep - 9:30 p.m.
```

_____

6.
```
get up - 6:30 a.m.
breakfast - 7:00 a.m.
go to school - 8:30 a.m.
lunch - 12:30 p.m.
finish school - 3:00 p.m.
dinner - 6.30 p.m.
watch TV - 7:30 p.m.
homework - 8:00 p.m.
sleep - 9:30 p.m.
```

_____

E　You are conducting a survey to find out what time your friends get up, have breakfast, have dinner, do their homework and go to bed. Write the five questions you need for the survey. Check the questions and interview your friends to complete the table.

Your questions:

1. _____

2. _____

3. _____

4. _____

5. _____

Names					
(yourself)					

Tell the class the results of your survey, including the number of people who do each activity earlier than you.

F Use complete sentences with as many characters as possible to write about your daily routine.

Example: 我早上七点半起床^{qǐchuáng}。

1. _____

2. _____

3. _____

4. _____

5. _____

6. _____

7. _____

8. _____

G Read the following story about 林国明 's father and answer the questions.

　　林国明的爸爸喜欢下棋（xiàqí）。今天上午，他七点半起床，七点四十五分吃早饭。八点，他和林国明下棋（xiàqí）。八点二十分，林国明去上学，他和林国明的哥哥下棋。九点半，哥哥去上班（shàngbān），他和妈妈下棋。十点四十五分，妈妈去买菜，他和朋友下棋。

　　十一点一刻（kè），他的朋友说："该吃午饭了。"他说："快十二点了吗？不，你的表快（biǎo kuài）了。下棋（xiàqí）！下棋（xiàqí）！"

　　十一点半，他的朋友说："嘿（hēi）！该（gāi）你了。"他说："是吗？啊（a）！快十二点了，该（gāi）吃午饭了。"

1. What's 林国明 's father's hobby?

2. Who did he play the game with and why did each one stop playing with him?

3. When did he stop the game and why? Give reasons for your answer.

H What should you say in Chinese in the following situations? Use complete sentences with as many characters as possible.

1. Tell someone it is his/her turn.

_____

2. Tell someone that he/she is late.

_____

3. Say sorry to someone because you are late.

_____

4. Tell someone that you like reading picture-story books.

_____

5. Urge someone to go in (somewhere, e. g. classroom, restaurant...)

_____

6. Tell someone that your watch is slow.

_____

7. Tell someone that his/her watch is fast.

_____

8. Say that things are in a terrible state.

_____

I Listen to the conversation between 王美怡 Wáng Měiyí and her mother then answer the following questions.

1. What time did 王美怡 Wáng Měiyí get up?

2. Why was she in such a hurry?

3. What is special about today?

4. What did 王美怡 Wáng Měiyí miss today? Why?

5. When is she coming home?

In the box below, paste the copy of the conversation given to you by your teacher to further check your understanding. Use this copy to hold a conversation with your partner.

dì sān kè　Xiǎomíng de jiā
第 三 课　小 明 的 家

A Listen to each description and choose the item that is normally put in the room described.

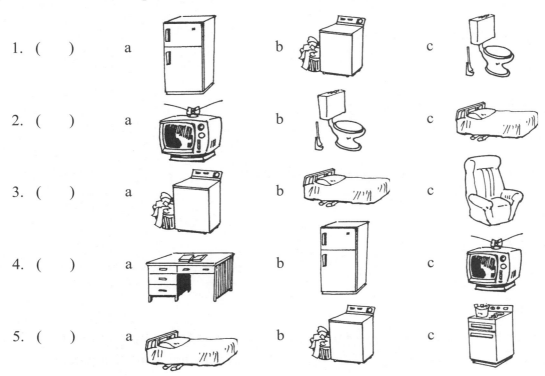

1. (　)　a　　　　b　　　　c

2. (　)　a　　　　b　　　　c

3. (　)　a　　　　b　　　　c

4. (　)　a　　　　b　　　　c

5. (　)　a　　　　b　　　　c

B Write the location of the following school objects according to their position relative to the schoolbag.

chǐ
1. 尺 _____

jiǎndāo
2. 剪刀 _____

xiàngpí
3. 橡皮 _____

4. 书 _____

máobǐ
5. 毛笔 _____

C You helped a Chinese neighbour to hide Easter eggs for their children to find. To make sure all will be found, write a note to remind him where the eggs are hidden.

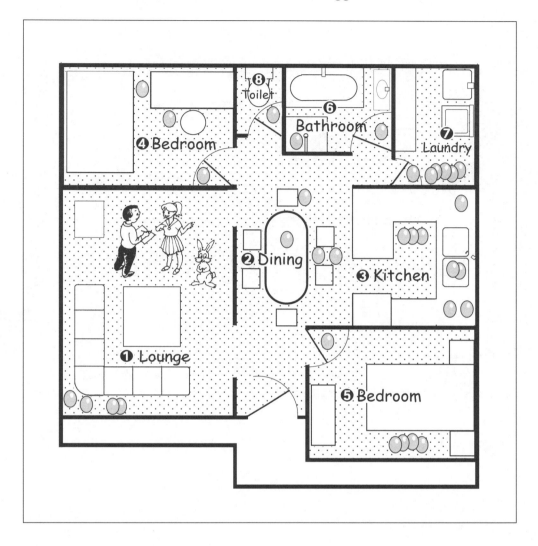

Your note:

1. e.g. 四个在客厅   2.＿＿＿＿＿＿＿＿   3.＿＿＿＿＿＿＿＿

4.＿＿＿＿＿＿＿＿   5.＿＿＿＿＿＿＿＿   6.＿＿＿＿＿＿＿＿

7.＿＿＿＿＿＿＿＿   8.＿＿＿＿＿＿＿＿

D 王美怡 Wáng Měiyí is looking for things in the house. Describe to her their relative locations, e.g. 在……上面 zài...shàngmian.

1. 我的书包在哪儿？
   ^{shūbāo}

   _____

2. 我的风筝在哪儿？
   ^{fēngzhēng}

   _____

3. 我的剪刀在哪里？
   ^{jiǎndāo}

   _____

4. 我的足球在哪里？
   ^{zúqiú}

   _____

5. 我们的电话呢？
   ^{diànhuà}

   _____

E These are the house plans of the following six people. Listen to each description and write the corresponding name under each one.

The six people: John, Wendy, Jeff, Christine, Charles, Susan.

1.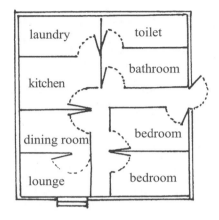

2.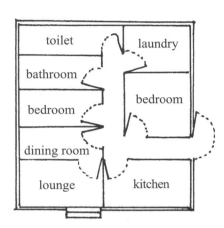

3.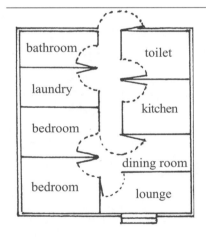

4.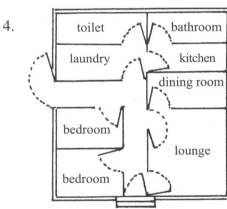

5.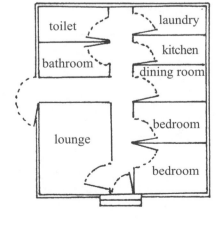

6.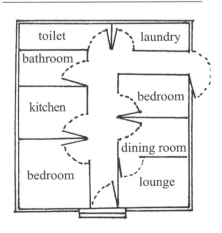

F Draw your house/unit plan and write a description of it. Tell the class about your house/unit.

G Choose from 新的 xīn de, 旧的 jiù de, 破了 pò le, 坏了 huài le and write the proper description for each item.

1.

_____

2.

_____

3.

_____

4.

_____

5.

_____

6.

_____

7.

_____

8.

_____

9.

_____

H Use the following characters to make as many words/phrases as possible. Write the meaning beside each word/phrase.

1. 生 _____ (　　　　　), _____ (　　　　　), _____ (　　　　　)

2. 上 _____ (　　　　　), _____ (　　　　　), _____ (　　　　　)

3. 下 _____ (　　　　　), _____ (　　　　　), _____ (　　　　　)

4. 前 _____ (　　　　　), _____ (　　　　　), _____ (　　　　　)

5. 后 _____ (　　　　　), _____ (　　　　　), _____ (　　　　　)

6. 左 _____ (　　　　　), _____ (　　　　　), _____ (　　　　　)

7. 今 _____ (　　　　　), _____ (　　　　　), _____ (　　　　　)

8. 明 _____ (　　　　　), _____ (　　　　　), _____ (　　　　　)

9. 电 _____ (　　　　　), _____ (　　　　　), _____ (　　　　　)

10. 看 _____ (　　　　　), _____ (　　　　　), _____ (　　　　　)

I Your family is moving to a new house, and you are responsible for keeping track of the following furniture. Write the number that corresponds to the item of furniture in the room where it should be placed. Describe the location of each item.

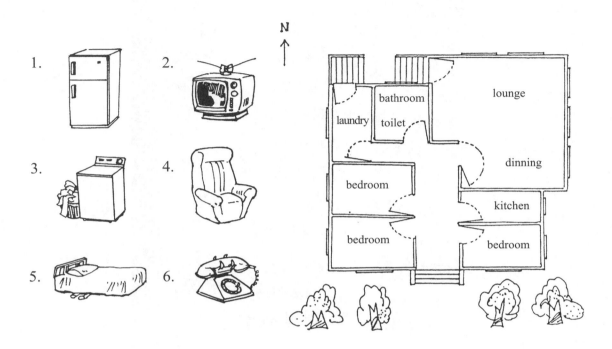

1. _____

2. _____

3. _____

4. _____

5. _____

6. _____

J　You are going to 上海 for an exchange study. This fax was sent to you by your hostess. Based on what can be read, draw her house plan and list her daily routine.

你好！
　欢迎你来上海。我们（家）是公寓。有两间卧室。客厅不大，在右边最前面。也不大，在客厅左边。是我的卧室。我的卧室不大，妈妈的卧室很大，在我卧室的对面。我卧室的后面，厕所在洗衣房旁边。
　我每天早上六点钟起床（六点半）吃早饭，七点上学。中午十二点我回家吃午饭，下午四点半放学。我们晚上七点吃饭，我们一家人都喜欢在电视机前面吃饭。八点半做功课，十点半睡觉。你……

王。我们家乐。我们的厨房看厨房后我爸爸洗衣房在旁边。

祝
王小华

House plan

Daily routine:

_____

_____

_____

_____

_____

K Listen to the conversation between 王美怡 Wáng Měiyí and her mother. Write the answers for the following questions.

1. When did 王美怡 Wáng Měiyí arrive home from school?

2. What was the first thing 王美怡 Wáng Měiyí did after coming home?

3. Did anything wrong happen? What was it?

4. What were the comments of Wáng Měiyí's mother during the conversation?

In the box below, paste the copy of the conversation given to you by your teacher to further check your understanding. Use this copy to hold a conversation with your partner.

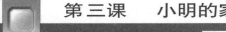

二十八

L Use the information given to complete the crosswords using Chinese characters.

Horizontal	Vertical
1. It is now 12:25.	10. What's the matter?
2. January	11. Where is (it)?
3. what	12. tomorrow
4. inside	13. February
5. come back	14. (It) is not me.
6. Tuesday	15. yours
7. 18 years old	16. 23 November
8. (It) is you.	17. May
9. Today is my birthday.	18. How old is she?

dì sì kè　wǒ de yīfu
第四课　我的衣服

A Listen to the description and choose the appropriate answer.

1. (　　) a b c

2. (　　) a b c

3. (　　) a b c

4. (　　) a b c

5. (　　) a b c

6. (　　) a b c

7. (　　) a b c

8. (　　) a   b c

9. (　　) a b c

10. (　　) a b c

B Listen to the description of the clothes worn by members of 王美怡 Wáng Měiyí's family. Draw lines connecting the person to the clothes he/she is wearing.

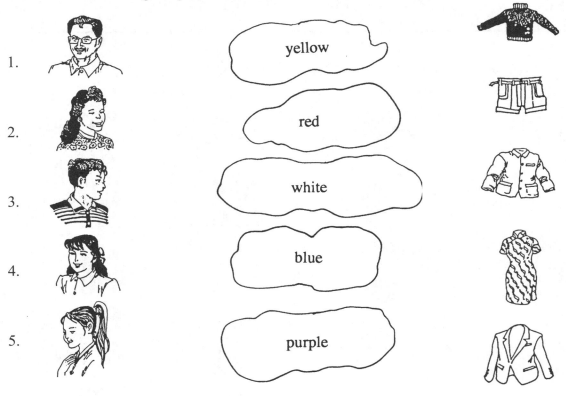

1.

2.

3.

4.

5.

yellow

red

white

blue

purple

Write a sentence, including measure words, to describe the clothes each person is wearing.

1. _____

2. _____

3. _____

4. _____

5. _____

C Draw a line from each Chinese description to the appropriate picture. Write a complete sentence in Chinese describing how the clothes fit each person.

1. 太肥了　　　　　_____

2. 很时髦　　　　　_____

3. 太长了　　　　　_____

4. 很漂亮　　　　　_____

5. 太大了　　　　　_____

6. 很合身　　　　　_____

7. 太瘦了　　　　　_____

8. 太小了　　　　　_____

9. 很舒服　　　　　_____

10. 太短了　　　　　_____

三十二

D Answer the following questions in complete sentences, using as many characters as possible.

1. 你的书包是什么颜色 (colour) 的？
_{shūbāo} _{yánsè}

_____

2. 你今天穿什么衣服？

_____

3. 你今天穿什么颜色的鞋子？
_{yánsè} _{xiézi}

_____

4. 你的袜子是什么颜色的？
_{wàzi} _{yánsè}

_____

5. 你们的汉语老师今天穿什么衣服？
_{Hànyǔ}

_____

6. 你看他的衣服怎么样？
_{zěnmeyàng}

_____

7. 你看这件衬衫怎么样？
_{chènshān zěnmeyàng}

_____

E Answer the following questions according to your own situation. Use complete sentences with as many characters as possible.

1. 你昨天有没有上学？

_____

2. 你今天有没有穿外套？
　　　　　　　　wàitào

_____

3. 你今天有没有吃早饭？

_____

4. 你今天早上有没有迟到？
　　　　　　　　　　chídào

_____

5. 你昨天晚上有没有做功课？
　　　　　　　　　　　gōngkè

_____

6. 你昨天晚上有没有看电视？
　　　　　　　　　　　diànshì

_____

7. 你上星期日有没有去看电影？
　　　　　　　　　　　　diànyǐng

_____

F Listen to the conversation between 王美怡 Wáng Měiyí and 林芳 Lín Fāng and write, on the drawing, the name of each person. Check your answers and then write a description of each person's outfit using complete sentences.

1. _____

2. _____

3. _____

4. _____

5. _____

G Read the following article about 黄蓝 and answer the questions.

黄蓝的衣服很多，也都很时髦。她有四条短裙，六条长裤和十件衬衫，有黑色和红色的，也有黄色和白色的。

今天她穿了一件黑色的衬衫，一条白色的长裤。她爸爸看到她，说："喔！你今天穿的衣服真合身，真漂亮。"她妈妈看到她，说："嘿！你的衬衫太短、太合身了。你的长裤上面太瘦、下面太肥了。"

1. What variety of clothes does 黄蓝 have?

2. What is she wearing today?

3. What opinions did she receive from her parents?

H Listen to the conversation between 王美怡 Wáng Měiyí and 林芳 Lín Fāng and answer the following questions.

1. What colour skirt is 王美怡 Wáng Měiyí wearing?

2. Is her skirt new? Give reasons for your answer.

3. How does the skirt fit her?

4. What is 林芳 Lín Fāng wearing today?

5. Are 林芳 Lín Fāng's clothes new? Give reasons for your answer.

In the box below, paste the copy of the conversation given to you by your teacher to further check your understanding. Use this copy to hold a conversation with your partner.

dì　wǔ　kè　　mǎi　dōngxi
第 五 课 　买 东 西

A　Rewrite the following price labels in Chinese.

1.　¥2.30 　＿＿＿＿＿＿＿＿＿＿＿＿

2.　¥8.00 　＿＿＿＿＿＿＿＿＿＿＿＿

3.　¥14.50 　＿＿＿＿＿＿＿＿＿＿＿＿

4.　¥70.00 　＿＿＿＿＿＿＿＿＿＿＿＿

5.　¥25.00 　＿＿＿＿＿＿＿＿＿＿＿＿

6.　¥99.00 　＿＿＿＿＿＿＿＿＿＿＿＿

7.　¥69.50 　＿＿＿＿＿＿＿＿＿＿＿＿

8.　¥8.60 　＿＿＿＿＿＿＿＿＿＿＿＿

9.　¥3.05 　＿＿＿＿＿＿＿＿＿＿＿＿

10.　¥9.80 　＿＿＿＿＿＿＿＿＿＿＿＿

11.　¥26.09 　＿＿＿＿＿＿＿＿＿＿＿＿

12.　¥0.75 　＿＿＿＿＿＿＿＿＿＿＿＿

13.　¥4.85 　＿＿＿＿＿＿＿＿＿＿＿＿

14.　¥0.50 　＿＿＿＿＿＿＿＿＿＿＿＿

15.　¥17.99 　＿＿＿＿＿＿＿＿＿＿＿＿

16.　¥0.05 　＿＿＿＿＿＿＿＿＿＿＿＿

17.　¥25.95 　＿＿＿＿＿＿＿＿＿＿＿＿

18.　¥13.10 　＿＿＿＿＿＿＿＿＿＿＿＿

19.　¥19.01 　＿＿＿＿＿＿＿＿＿＿＿＿

20.　¥99.99 　＿＿＿＿＿＿＿＿＿＿＿＿

B Listen to the conversations and choose the fruit that is mentioned in each.

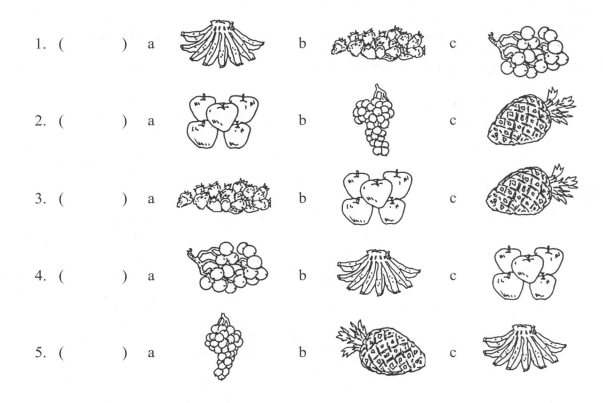

1. (　　) a　　　　b　　　　c

2. (　　) a　　　　b　　　　c

3. (　　) a　　　　b　　　　c

4. (　　) a　　　　b　　　　c

5. (　　) a　　　　b　　　　c

C In the fruit shop, label each item and its price in Chinese. Use as many characters as possible.

D Six people are going to buy fruit. Unfortunately, the stock is limited in all the stores. Listen to each person's description and write his/her name under the store that can supply everything he/she needs.

1.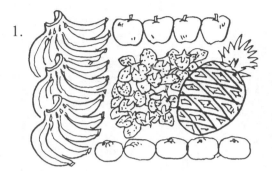

_____

2.

_____

3.

_____

4.

_____

5.

_____

6.

_____

E You did some shopping for a Chinese family. The following is what you bought. Write a report to the family giving the cost of each item and the total cost. Use complete sentences in your report with as many characters as possible.

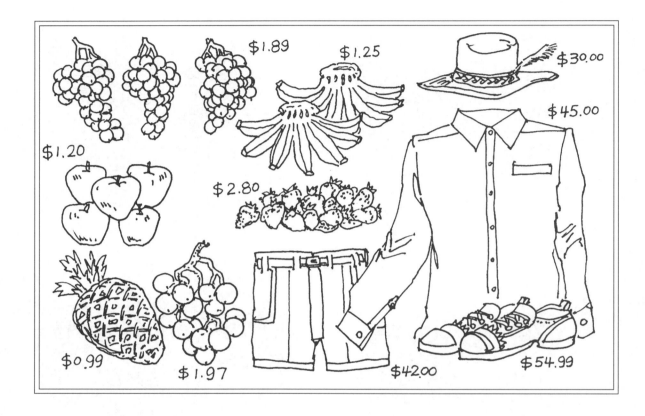

F Imagine that you are buying things in a Chinese department store. What would you say in the following situations? Write your answers in complete sentences using as many characters as possible.

1. You would like to find out if there is a 棉袄 mián'ǎo for sale.

_____

2. You like it in blue.

_____

3. It is too big. You would like to know if they have a smaller size.

_____

4. You feel that it is pretty good and would like to know the price.

_____

5. You feel that it is fairly cheap and would like to buy that one.

_____

6. Tell the salesperson that you would also like to buy a pair of shoes.

_____

7. You feel that this pair is too expensive and would like to have a cheaper one.

_____

8. You would like to know the total cost of the 棉袄 mián'ǎo and the shoes.

_____

G Read the story about 林国明 's shopping trip and answer the questions.

林国明的裤子^{kùzi}太小了，他妈妈给了他一百块，叫他去买一条新裤子^{tiáo xīn kùzi}。

今天下午他去百货商店^{bǎihuò shāngdiàn}，看到一条黄裤子^{tiáo kùzi}，一件白汗衫^{hànshān}，

他都很喜欢。百货商店^{bǎihuò shāngdiàn}的黄小姐说，裤子^{kùzi}四十七块五，

汗衫^{hànshān}三十九块六，一共八十六块一。林国明给她一百块，

她找了二十三块九毛。林国明想："不对吧？"他回去找

黄小姐。

1. What did 林国明 buy and why did he buy them?

2. What was the cost and how much was he charged?

3. What should he say to the shopkeeper when he returned? Write your answer in Chinese.

H You and your partner play the parts of a shopkeeper and a customer. Decide what to buy and write your conversation. Check the correctness, practise your conversation and have role-play in class.

_____ : _____

_____ : _____

_____ : _____

_____ : _____

_____ : _____

_____ : _____

_____ : _____

_____ : _____

_____ : _____

I In the following descriptions, state the levels of degree, indicating extremely, very, not very, not and not at all.

好 ＿＿＿＿＿＿＿＿＿＿　＿＿＿＿＿＿＿＿＿＿　＿＿＿＿＿＿＿＿＿＿

＿＿＿＿＿＿＿＿＿＿　＿＿＿＿＿＿＿＿＿＿

xīn
新 ＿＿＿＿＿＿＿＿＿＿　＿＿＿＿＿＿＿＿＿＿　＿＿＿＿＿＿＿＿＿＿

＿＿＿＿＿＿＿＿＿＿　＿＿＿＿＿＿＿＿＿＿

jiù
旧 ＿＿＿＿＿＿＿＿＿＿　＿＿＿＿＿＿＿＿＿＿　＿＿＿＿＿＿＿＿＿＿

＿＿＿＿＿＿＿＿＿＿　＿＿＿＿＿＿＿＿＿＿

piányi
便宜 ＿＿＿＿＿＿＿＿＿＿　＿＿＿＿＿＿＿＿＿＿　＿＿＿＿＿＿＿＿＿＿

＿＿＿＿＿＿＿＿＿＿　＿＿＿＿＿＿＿＿＿＿

guì
贵 ＿＿＿＿＿＿＿＿＿＿　＿＿＿＿＿＿＿＿＿＿　＿＿＿＿＿＿＿＿＿＿

＿＿＿＿＿＿＿＿＿＿　＿＿＿＿＿＿＿＿＿＿

suān
酸 ＿＿＿＿＿＿＿＿＿＿　＿＿＿＿＿＿＿＿＿＿　＿＿＿＿＿＿＿＿＿＿

＿＿＿＿＿＿＿＿＿＿　＿＿＿＿＿＿＿＿＿＿

tián
甜 ＿＿＿＿＿＿＿＿＿＿　＿＿＿＿＿＿＿＿＿＿　＿＿＿＿＿＿＿＿＿＿

＿＿＿＿＿＿＿＿＿＿　＿＿＿＿＿＿＿＿＿＿

J　Rewrite the following using " 的 "

1. the people who are going to the movie _____

2. the people who have had dinner _____

3. the movie that starts at 8 o'clock _____

4. the person who wears a red shirt _____

5. the apples bought yesterday _____

6. We went to the movie that started at 11:00 this morning.

_____

7. The one who wears the black skirt is my sister.

_____

8. The pineapple you bought this morning is sour.

_____

9. I would like a smaller dictionary.

_____

10. He is wearing brown trousers today.

_____

K Listen to the conversation between 王美怡 Wáng Měiyí and her mother and answer the following questions.

1. Where did 王美怡 Wáng Měiyí's mother go this morning?

2. What is 王美怡 Wáng Měiyí's favourite fruit?

3. Are the lychees good today? How much are they?

4. Compare the prices of the fruit the mother bought today.

In the box below, paste the copy of the conversation given to you by your teacher to further check your understanding. Use this copy to hold a conversation with your partner.

dì liù kè   bàifǎng péngyou
第 六 课　拜 访 朋 友

A Here is your schedule for the holiday week. Answer the following questions according to your schedule. Give reasons if you are not free.

May

Mon 12	Tue 13	Wed 14	Thu 15	Fri 16	Sat 17	Sun 18
go fishing with dad	9:00 - 11:45 a.m. football with friends	7:00 p.m. movie with friends	dinner in a restaurant with family		a.m. swimming with Xiaolan	

1. 你星期一有空吗？

_____

2. 你星期二上午有空吗？

_____

3. 你星期三下午有空吗？

_____

4. 你星期四晚上有没有空？

_____

5. 小兰五月十七号有空吗？

_____

6. 你五月十八号有没有空？

_____

B Tell the class where these people live according to the information given on the maps. Then answer the following questions.

Xiǎolán
1. 小兰住哪里？

_____

Xiǎolì
2. 小丽住哪儿？

_____

Lín
3. 林大中住哪儿？

_____

4. Peter 住哪儿？

_____

5. Sharon 住哪里？

_____

6. Ben 住哪里？

_____

7. Clinton 住哪儿？

_____

8. Bob 住哪里？

_____

C Tell the class where these people live and their telephone numbers according to the information given. Write your answers using as many characters as possible.

Name	Address & telephone number	Name	Address & telephone number
Mr. Li	12 Queen St, Chicago. Tel: 33872294	Mrs. Li	123 York St, Sydney. Tel: 22540921
Miss Li	25 Chang'an St, Beijing. Tel: 652371	Mr. Lin	1 Red St, San Francisco. Tel: 6518720
Miss Lin	123 Main St, New York. Tel: 4846537	Mr. Bai	20 Spencer St, Melbourne. Tel: 7601483

1. 李先生住哪儿？

_____

2. 李太太的电话号码是多少？

_____

3. 林小姐住哪儿？

_____

4. 林先生的电话是多少？

_____

5. 李小姐住哪儿？她的电话是多少？

_____

6. 白先生住哪儿？他的电话是多少？

_____

D　Where do 林芳 Lín Fāng's family members and friends of her parents work? Answer the questions according to the information given.

1. 爸爸在哪儿工作？
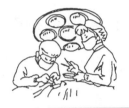

_____

2. 妈妈在哪儿工作？

_____

3. 哥哥在哪儿工作？

_____

4. 姐姐在哪儿工作？

_____

5. 李叔叔在哪儿工作？

_____

6. 白阿姨在哪儿上班？

_____

7. 林叔叔在哪儿上班？

_____

E Imagine that you are visiting 林芳 Lín Fāng. What do you say in the following situations? Write your answers using complete sentences with as many characters as possible.

1. Introduce yourself when a boy answers the door.

_____

2. You would like to know if your friend 林芳 Lín Fāng is home.

_____

3. You would like to know if the boy is 林芳 Lín Fāng's older brother.

_____

4. You need to apologise to your friend for being late.

_____

5. You greet your friend's mother when introduced to her.

_____

6. You are offered something to drink by your friend's mother.

_____

7. Thank your friend's mother before you leave.

_____

8. Thank your friend's mother when she invites you to have dinner with them.

_____

F Match the question and answer in each conversation and write them below.

1. 你找谁？　　　　　　　有^a啊！有什么事吗？

2. 请问，林大中在家吗？　好的。谢谢您。

3. 你住哪儿？　　　　　　吃了。谢谢。

4. 你父亲(fùqin)在哪儿工作？　在，他在吃饭。我去叫他。

5. 吃饭了吗？　　　　　　哪里！不用客气(kèqi)。

6. 有空常(cháng)来玩儿。　我找王美怡(Wáng Měiyí)。请问她在家吗？

7. 今天太打扰(dǎrǎo)您了。　他在银行(yínháng)上班。

8. 你明天有空吗？　　　　我住悉尼(Xīní)。

1. _____

2. _____

3. _____

4. _____

5. _____

6. _____

7. _____

8. _____

G Read the story about 林国明 's day and answer the questions.

　　星期六林国明去黄进家找他玩儿。他上午十一点半到黄进家。黄进不在家。他妈妈在家。他妈妈说黄进去书店（shūdiàn）买一本杂志（zázhì），马上回来。她请林国明到客厅（kètīng）坐，还请他喝茶（chá）。她问林国明住哪儿，家里有几个人，哥哥上几年级，妹妹今年几岁，父亲（fùqin）、母亲（mǔqin）在哪儿工作（gōngzuò）……。

　　十二点一刻（kè），黄进回来了。黄进的妈妈请林国明在他们家吃午饭。吃了午饭，他们一起（yìqǐ）去学校（xuéxiào）打网球（wǎngqiú）和游泳（yóuyǒng），玩得很过瘾（guòyǐn）。

1. Who did 林国明 visit and when did he arrive?

2. Who answered the door and how was he received?

3. Do you think 林国明 enjoyed his day today? Give reasons to your answer.

H　Listen to the conversation between 王美怡 Wáng Měiyí and 李大中 Lǐ Dàzhōng and answer the following questions.

1. What does 王美怡 Wáng Měiyí plan to do on Saturday?

2. When is she available?

3. Why is 李大中 Lǐ Dàzhōng visiting 王美怡 Wáng Měiyí?

4. What does 王美怡 Wáng Měiyí plan to do on Sunday?

5. When will 李大中 Lǐ Dàzhōng arrive on Sunday?

In the box below, paste the copy of the conversation given to you by your teacher to further check your understanding. Use this copy to hold a conversation with your partner.

I Based on the information given in section H, imagine that you are 李大中 Lǐ Dàzhōng who visited 王美怡 Wáng Měiyí today. Describe 王美怡 Wáng Měiyí's house and your visit in your diary.

A　A guide is talking to the member of a Chinese tourist group during a free period. Listen to their conversation and choose the correct answer.

1. ( )　　a. Dahua is coming back at 8:00 in the morning.
　　　　　b. Dahua is coming back at 3:30 in the afternoon.
　　　　　c. Dahua is coming back at 8:00 in the evening.

2. ( )　　a. Meiling is coming back at 5:30 in the afternoon.
　　　　　b. Meiling is coming back at 5:15 in the afternoon.
　　　　　c. Meiling is coming back at 5:45 in the afternoon.

3. ( )　　a. Xiao Zhang is coming back at around 3:00 in the afternoon.
　　　　　b. Xiao Zhang is probably coming back at 3:00 in the morning.
　　　　　c. Xiao Zhang will not come back at 3:00 in the afternoon.

4. ( )　　a. Lily is coming back to have dinner.
　　　　　b. Lily will probably come back at noon.
　　　　　c. Lily will not come back to have lunch.

5. ( )　　a. Wendy is coming back alone at 4:30 p.m.
　　　　　b. Wendy and Mary are going shopping at 4:30 p.m.
　　　　　c. Wendy and Mary are both coming back at 4:30 p.m.

6. ( )　　a. John is coming back at 6:00 p.m.
　　　　　b. John is coming back at 10:00 a.m.
　　　　　c. John is not going anywhere.

7. ( )　　a. Xiao Wang will come back at 11:30 in the evening.
　　　　　b. Xiao Wang will come back at 10:00 in the morning.
　　　　　c. Xiao Wang will come back at 10:00 in the evening.

8. ( )　　a. Miss Lin will come back at 3:00 p.m.
　　　　　b. Miss Lin will not come back at 3:00 p.m.
　　　　　c. Miss Lin will go out at 3:00 p.m.

9. ( )　　a. Mr. White is going out immediately.
　　　　　b. Mr. White is coming back right away.
　　　　　c. Mr. White is going out at 10:00 a.m.

10. ( )　　a. Mrs. Wang is going out to have dinner.
　　　　　b. Mrs. Wang is coming back at 6:00 p.m.
　　　　　c. Mrs. Wang is not having dinner.

B Answer the following questions according to the information given, using complete sentences with as many characters as possible.

1. 请问，您是哪位？

_____

2. 请问，你找谁？

_____

3. 请问，您找哪位？

_____

4. 请问，您打的是多少号？

_____

5. 请问是七二四九一〇六吗？

_____

6. 请问是九三二〇七六八吗？

_____

7. 白老师在不在家？

_____

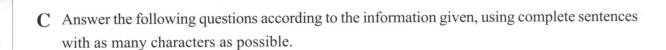

C Answer the following questions according to the information given, using complete sentences with as many characters as possible.

1. 白老师要去书店做什么？　shūdiàn

_____

2. 王太太要去市场买什么？　Wáng shìchǎng

_____

3. 王小姐要去百货商店买什么？　Wáng bǎihuò shāngdiàn

_____

4. 林先生要去黄金海岸干什么？　Lín Huángjīn Hǎi'àn gàn

to have fun

_____

5. 林太太要去中国城干什么？　Lín gàn

_____

6. 王先生要去旧金山干什么？　Wáng Jiùjīnshān gàn

_____

7. 小弟弟星期日要去学校做什么？　xuéxiào

_____

D Match the question and answer in each conversation and write them below.

1. 请问，王^{Wáng}先生在家吗？　　　是的，您找哪位？

2. 您找哪位？　　　　　　　　　　对不起，他出去了。

3. 你的电话是多少？　　　　　　　可以。你要买什么？

4. 请问，你打的是多少号？　　　　对不起，我明天很忙^{máng}。

5. 您打错号码^{hàomǎ}了！　　　　　　我打的是六一〇五七八三^{yāo}。

6. 请问是六四三五九二〇吗？　　　我的电话是九一^{yāo}六五四三七。

7. 你下午可以和我去买东西^{dōngxi}吗？　噢^ò！对不起。

8. 你明天有空吗？　　　　　　　我找王^{Wáng}先生。

1. _____

2. _____

3. _____

4. _____

5. _____

6. _____

7. _____

8. _____

E Imagine that you are answering or making a phone call. What do you say in the following situations? Write your answers using as many characters as possible.

1. You answer the phone and hear some Chinese. It is obviously a wrong number.

_____

2. You explain that your phone number is 5432106, not 5423106.

_____

3. You call your Australian friend John, but hear people answer in Chinese.

_____

4. You would like to know if Lee is at home.

_____

5. You answer the phone and it is your friend's father, Mr. Li.

_____

6. Mr. Li asks to talk to your father over the phone.

_____

7. Mr. Li says that you speak Chinese very well.

_____

8. Your Chinese friend's mother calls you on the phone.

_____

F　Rearrange the characters in each question to make a sentence.

1. 了间不时早，该了我走。

_____

2. 书这钱三共本一多少？

_____

3. 住儿你哪？多话是电少？

_____

4. 不对起，你一请下等。

_____

5. 今服该呢穿我什衣天么？

_____

6. 上你有明吗午空天？

_____

7. 电你回我后请打家话给。

_____

8. 天去到学我家同玩儿昨。

_____

G Write the following signs in Chinese to display around the school.

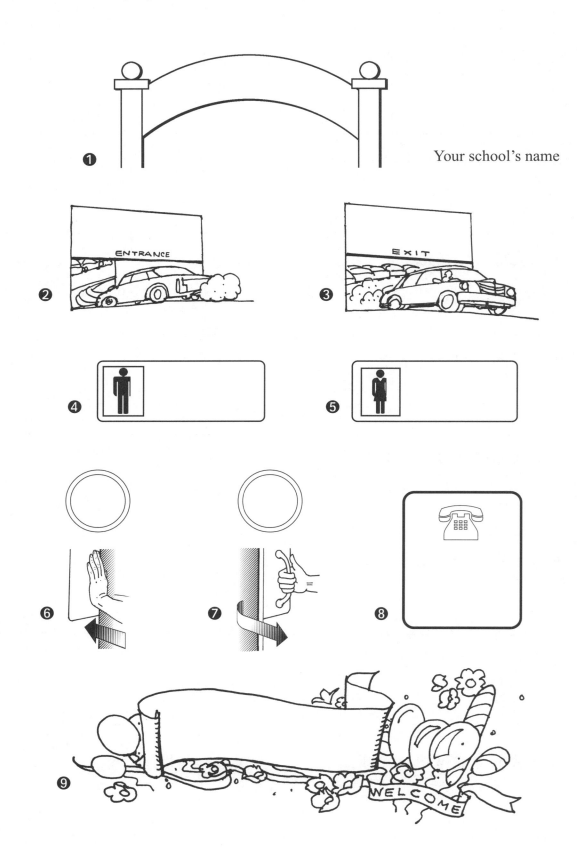

Your school's name

H Listen to the conversation between 王美怡 Wáng Měiyí and 林芳 Lín Fāng and answer the following questions.

1. Where did 王美怡 Wáng Měiyí go last night?

2. What time did 林芳 Lín Fāng ring 王美怡 Wáng Měiyí? Why was her call not answered?

3. List the people who were home in 王美怡 Wáng Měiyí's family.

4. What is 王美怡 Wáng Měiyí's phone number?

In the box below, paste the copy of the conversation given to you by your teacher to further check your understanding. Use this copy to hold a conversation with your partner.

六十四

I Read the following paragraph about 林国明's phone call then answer the questions.

今天林国明打电话找 Peter。接电话的是一位小姐，她

说："她不在家。"林国明问："请问，他什么时候回来？"

她说："她和妈妈去百货商店，她想买一条连衣裙。她们

大概下午五点左右回来。"林国明问："Peter 为什么要买

连衣裙？是给他的女朋友吗？Peter 没有女朋友啊！"小

姐说："你是找 Peter，还是 Peta？我们家有 Peta，没有

Peter。你打的是多少号？"林国明回答："我打的是九八

一四九七三。"小姐说："你打错了，我们的电话是九

八一四六三七。"

1. Who did 林国明 call and what message did he receive?

2. What does "女朋友" mean?

3. What confused 林国明 about his friend and what was the truth?

A You are visiting your Chinese friend 国明 Guómíng. You would like to invite him to go to a movie with you next Saturday afternoon. As Guómíng just went fishing with his father, you are leaving him a note. Write your note using as many characters as possible. Do not forget to ask him to call you.

B What do you say in the following situations? Use 因为 yīnwèi... 所以 suǒyǐ... in your sentences.

1. You do not like sweet and sour pork because it is too sweet.

_____

2. You do not like the pineapple because it is too sour.

_____

3. You do not like to wear the shirt because it does not fit well.

_____

4. You like these grapes because they are very sweet.

_____

5. You did not do your homework because you went to a movie last night.

_____

6. You are late for school because you slept in this morning.

_____

7. You are very hungry now because you did not have breakfast this morning.

_____

8. You like your mother's cooking because she cooks well.

_____

C You are conducting a survey with some friends to find out: 1. if they often go to Chinese restaurants, 2. if they like yumcha, 3. if they often eat Chinese food at home, and 4. their favourite dishes. Write the four questions you need for the survey and interview eight friends to complete the table. Check your questions before your survey and report your results to the class after your survey.

Your questions:

1. _____

2. _____

3. _____

4. _____

Names		Yumcha		
Comments				

D You and your family are going to a Chinese restaurant for dinner. Write your favourites below and tell your class about your choice.

Entree (Appetizer):

_____

_____

Soup:

_____

_____

Main course:

_____

_____

_____

Rice:

_____

Dessert (selection of fruit):

_____

E   You are in a Chinese restaurant. What do you say to the waiter in the following situations?

1. You ask the waiter for the menu.

_____

2. You explain to the waiter that you are ordering today because it is your birthday.

_____

3. You order the lemon chicken and mapo bean curd, no soup.

_____

4. You would like to have plain rice.

_____

5. You do not want to have MSG in your food.

_____

6. You tell the waiter that the lemon chicken is a bit too sour.

_____

7. You tell the restaurant owner that the food is great.

_____

8. You ask for the bill.

_____

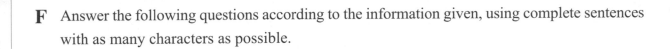

F Answer the following questions according to the information given, using complete sentences with as many characters as possible.

1. 她喜欢吃冰淇淋还是水果？
_{bīngqílín}　_{shuǐguǒ}

_____

2. 他喜欢吃米饭还是炒饭？
_{mǐfàn}　_{chǎofàn}

_____

3. 她住洋房还是公寓？
_{yángfáng}　_{gōngyù}

_____

4. 她们在打乒乓球还是打网球？
_{pīngpāngqiú}　_{wǎngqiú}

_____

5. 她在做功课还是看小人儿书？
_{gōngkè}

_____

6. 这条裙子太肥还是太瘦？
_{tiáo qúnzi}　_{féi}　_{shòu}

_____

7. 这是五块钱还是五毛钱？

_____

G You are invited by a Chinese friend to have dinner at his/her home. Here are parts of the conversation you will have with your friend's family. Write your responses using as many characters as possible.

1. 来，请喝果汁。
_{guǒzhī}

_____

2. 你住哪儿？

_____

3. 你父亲在哪儿工作？
_{fùqin}　　_{gōngzuò}

_____

4. 吃饭了。来，你坐这儿。

_____

5. 没什么菜，你自己来。

_____

6. 你常吃中国菜吗？

_____

7. 这菜好吃。来，多吃点儿。

_____

8. 要不要再添一碗饭？
_{tiān}　_{wǎn}

_____

H Choose the best word for each question. Then use each word to make a sentence of your own.

| 尤其
yóuqí | 还是 | 客气 | 常常 | 客人 | 一起 | 回来 | 平常 |

1. 他出去了？请问他什么时候 _____？

　 _____

2. 你喜欢游泳 _____ 喜欢打球？

　 _____

3. 来，自己来，别 ^{bié} _____。

　 _____

4. 我哥哥星期六 _____ 不在家。

　 _____

5. 他喜欢打球，_____ 喜欢打板球 ^{bǎnqiú}。

　 _____

6. 今天我们家有很多 _____。

　 _____

7. 我 _____ 都很早到，可是今天迟到 ^{chídào} 了。

　 _____

8. 明天我想到书店去，你要不要和我 _____ 去？

　 _____

I Read the following story about 林国明 's outing and answer the questions.

　　上个星期天中午，林国明和同学黄平一起去中国城。他们想去饮茶，可是因为要饮茶的人太多了，所以他们去了一家小馆子。他们点了两盘^{pán}炒饭，一大碗^{wǎn}豆腐汤^{dòufu tāng}。豆腐汤做得还不错，炒饭也很好吃，他们都吃得很饱^{bǎo}。这家馆子的菜不贵，两盘^{pán}炒饭和豆腐汤^{dòufu tāng}一共九块四。黄平说今天中午他请客。

　　吃过午饭，他们在一家书店^{shūdiàn}看到一些^{yìxiē}旧^{jiù}杂志^{zázhì}，很便宜^{piányi}，六本五块钱。林国明买了十二本。他问黄平喜不喜欢看杂志^{zázhì}，黄平说喜欢，所以他给了黄平六本。

1. When and where did 林国明 go ? Who did he go with?

2. What did they plan to eat and what did they end up eating?

3. Did they enjoy the food? Why?

4. How much did each of them spend and what did they spend it on?

J 王美怡 Wáng Měiyí and 李大中 Lǐ Dàzhōng met on the road. Listen to their conversation and answer the following questions.

1. Where was 王美怡 Wáng Měiyí going?

2. When did 李大中 Lǐ Dàzhōng visit her and what happened?

3. Why did 李大中 Lǐ Dàzhōng visit 王美怡 Wáng Měiyí?

4. What was special about yesterday?

5. Does 王美怡 Wáng Měiyí often go to Chinese restaurants?

In the box below, paste the copy of the conversation given to you by your teacher to further check your understanding. Use this copy to hold a conversation with your partner.

dì   jiǔ   kè   tiānqì
第 九 课　天 气

A Listen and choose the weather that is mentioned in each statement.

1. (　　　) a　　　　　　b　　　　　　c

2. (　　　) a　　　　　　b　　　　　　c

3. (　　　) a　　　　　　b　　　　　　c

4. (　　　) a 　　b　　　　　　c

5. (　　　) a 　　b　　　　　　c

6. (　　　) a　　　　　　b　　　　　　c

7. (　　　) a 　　b　　　　　　c

8. (　　　) a　　　　　　b 　　c

9. (　　　) a　　　　　　b　　　　　　c

10. (　　　) a　　　　　　b 　　c

B This is today's forecast from the weather bureau. Answer the following questions according to the information given.

| Sydney: shower, 2, 10 | Beijing, clear, 29, 35 | San Francisco: cloudy, 20, 28 |

Xīní
1. 悉尼今天的天气怎么样？

_____

Xīní
2. 悉尼今天下雨吗？

_____

3. 北京今天的天气很冷还是很热？

_____

4. 北京今天有没有下雪？

_____

Jiùjīnshān
5. 旧金山今天的天气怎么样？

_____

Jiùjīnshān
6. 旧金山今天很热吗？

_____

C Answer the following questions according to the information given, using complete sentences with as many characters as possible.

1. 昨天天气怎么样？

_____

2. 北京今天下雪吗？

_____

3. 你看明天的天气怎么样？

_____

4. 你看下午会下雨吗？

_____

5. 你看后天会不会刮大风？

_____

6. 你今天下午会不会去游泳？

_____

^{Wáng}
7. 王叔叔明天会来吗？

_____

七十八

D 张明 Zhāng Míng lives in northeast China 东北 Dōngběi, where the weather is cold and summer is short. Listen and take brief notes of his description of the four seasons there. Check your notes and write a full description in Chinese, using as many characters as possible.

Notes -

　　Spring:

　　Summer:

　　Autumn:

　　Winter:

Your description:

_____

_____

_____

_____

_____

_____

E Describe, using as many characters as possible, the duration of the seasons and the climate of each season in your city.

八十

F Listen to the weather report for various cities and draw lines from each city to the corresponding descriptions. Check your answers and then write your own report in Chinese.

	Condition	Min temp.	Max temp.
Beijing	cloudy	22	16
Taipei	fine, afternoon shower	2	9
Melbourne	clear	0	10
New York	fine, sometimes cloudy	20	31
San Francisco	rainy	8	34

_____ : _____

_____

_____ : _____

_____

_____ : _____

_____

_____ : _____

_____

_____ : _____

_____

G How do you say the following in Chinese? Use complete sentences with as many characters as possible.

1. How's the weather today?

_____

2. What's the maximum temperature today?

_____

3. The minimum temperature was 5˚C yesterday.

_____

4. The weather forecast said there is going to be a storm this afternoon.

_____

5. It snowed last night.

_____

6. Is it still raining now?

_____

7. It is going to be a hot day tomorrow.

_____

8. It is cool and pleasant here in Spring, but very windy in Autumn.

_____

H 王美怡 Wáng Měiyí and 李大中 Lǐ Dàzhōng are talking about the weather. Listen to their conversation and answer the following questions.

1. Is it likely to snow today? Give reasons for your answer.

2. What is the temperature now?

3. What did 王美怡 Wáng Měiyí think about the weather?

4. What type of weather does 李大中 Lǐ Dàzhōng dislike?

In the box below, paste the copy of the conversation given to you by your teacher to further check your understanding. Use this copy to hold a conversation with your partner.

I Use the following characters to make as many words/phrases as possible. Write the meaning beside each word/phrase.

1. 上 _____ (   ), _____ (   ), _____ (   ), _____ (   )

2. 中 _____ (   ), _____ (   ), _____ (   ), _____ (   )

3. 下 _____ (   ), _____ (   ), _____ (   ), _____ (   )

4. 学 _____ (   ), _____ (   ), _____ (   ), _____ (   )

5. 客 _____ (   ), _____ (   ), _____ (   ), _____ (   )

6. 气 _____ (   ), _____ (   ), _____ (   ), _____ (   )

7. 常 _____ (   ), _____ (   ), _____ (   ), _____ (   )

8. 时 _____ (   ), _____ (   ), _____ (   ), _____ (   )

9. 饭 _____ (   ), _____ (   ), _____ (   ), _____ (   )

10. 么 _____ (   ), _____ (   ), _____ (   ), _____ (   )

11. 为 _____ (   ), _____ (   ), _____ (   ), _____ (   )

12. 回 _____ (   ), _____ (   ), _____ (   ), _____ (   )

J This is a diary entry of 王美怡 Wáng Měiyí. Read her diary and answer the questions.

二〇〇一年十一月二十九日　　上午晴，下午雷阵雨 (léizhènyǔ)

昨天早上的气温(qìwēn)是摄氏(Shèshì)二十三度左右，可是今天上午十一点，气温(qìwēn)是摄氏四十一度。对面的一家人有游泳池(chí)，他们都在游泳池(chí)里玩水。我们家没有游泳池，我和妹妹穿游泳衣在浴室(yùshì)里玩水。中午我们吃了三份(fèn)冰淇淋(bīngqílín)，没吃饭。下午一点半，妹妹说外面看起来好像(hǎoxiàng)要下雨。两点左右，下了大雨，又刮了大风。

现在是四点一刻(kè)，雨停(tíng)了，可是还有点儿风。我有点儿冷，妹妹说现在的气温(qìwēn)是十九度，她很冷，她要去穿一件外套(wàitào)，我说我也要去穿一件外套(wàitào)。

1. Describe in detail the change in today's weather and temperature.

2. How did 王美怡 adapt to the weather?

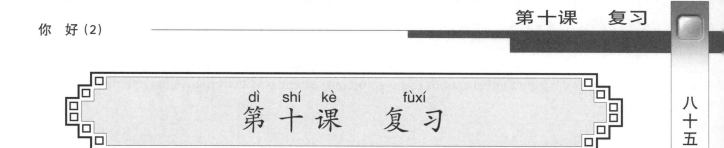

dì   shí   kè   fùxí
第 十 课　复 习

A It is Sunday night. This morning you went swimming with a Chinese friend. After swimming, your friend invited you home to have lunch. In your diary, write today's date and weather, what you had for lunch, what you did in the morning and in the afternoon and how your day was.

B Answer the following questions using complete sentences with as many characters as possible.

1. 今天是几月几号，星期几？

_____

2. 你是哪年生的？

_____

3. 你的生日是什么时候？

_____

^{Wáng}
4. 王先生在做什么？

_____

5. 你早上几点起床？
^{qǐchuáng}

_____

6. 小妹妹的剪刀在哪儿？
^{jiǎndāo}

_____

7. 小弟弟在客厅做什么？
^{kètīng}

_____

8. 这是怎么回事？

_____

C Answer the following questions using complete sentences with as many characters as possible.

1. 白老师今天穿什么衣服？

_____

2. 你看这顶帽子怎么样？
   dǐng　màozi

_____

3. 你昨天晚上有没有做功课？
   gōngkè

_____

4. 这本汉英字典多少钱？
   Hàn-Yīng zìdiǎn

_____

5. 这香蕉怎么卖？
   xiāngjiāo

_____

6. 这菠萝酸不酸？
   bōluó　suān

_____

7. 你下星期六有空吗？

_____

8. 你住哪儿？你家的电话是多少？

_____

D What do you say in Chinese in the following situations? Write your answers using as many characters as possible.

1. You would like to know who you are speaking to on the phone.

_____

2. You would like to know if John is at home.

_____

3. You would like to know when Peter is coming back.

_____

4. You would like to know why Susan is going to Chinatown.

_____

5. You explain that you are late because you slept in this morning.

_____

6. You say that it was hot yesterday, but it is cool today.

_____

7. You would like to know whether Paul likes summer or winter.

_____

8. You ask Jason if it is going to rain tomorrow.

_____

E Rearrange the characters in each question to make a sentence.

1. 老师爸爸我是，中学书在教^{jiāo}。

_____

2. 找林朋我，请他在问家不在？

_____

3. 城去中国玩儿要我们，三点回来左右下午。

_____

4. 吃他们星期常常炒饭天。

_____

5. 生日妈妈是因为的今天，饭馆我们所以吃饭去中国。

_____

6. 凉快的秋天很北京，很风大春天。

_____

7. 热夏天北京的很，很天冷冬。

_____

8. 今天太热的了天气，想我游泳去。

_____

F Listen to the conversation between 王美怡 Wáng Měiyí and 李大中 Lǐ Dàzhōng and answer the following questions.

1. Where did this conversation take place? Give reasons for your answer.

2. What time was it then?

3. When were they going to the movie?

4. What were they going to do before going to the cinema?

In the box below, paste the copy of the conversation given to you by your teacher to further check your understanding. Use this copy to hold a conversation with your partner.

Writing exercise

How to write a character correctly:

1. Write the strokes according to the numbered sequence.
2. Start each stroke beginning where the number is located.
3. End a stroke with the pen lifted off the paper if it has a pointy end, or with the pen stopped on the paper if it has a round end.

Trace the two lightly printed examples and maintain the proportions in the practice boxes.

The first space is for you to write the Pinyin and meaning of each character.

1 月	*Pinyin:* *Meaning:* 月 月							
日	P: M: 日 日							
号	P: M: 号 号							
今	P: M: 今 今							
明	P: M: 明 明							
昨	P: M: 昨 昨							
天	P: M: 天 天							

九十二

星	P: M:								
星	星 星								
期	P: M:								
	期 期								
对	P: M:								
	对 对								
错	P: M:								
	错 错								
可	P: M:								
	可 可								
以	P: M:								
	以 以								
行	P: M:								
	行 行								
生	P: M:								
	生 生								
在	P: M:								
	在 在								

2

做 P:
M:

做 做

看 P:
M:

看 看

书 P:
M:

书 书

写 P:
M:

写 写

字 P:
M:

字 字

现 P:
M:

现 现

点 P:
M:

点 点

分 P:
M:

分 分

半 P:
M:

半 半

3

了	P: M:							
	了	了						
下	P: M:							
	下	下						
午	P: M:							
	午	午						
早	P: M:							
	早	早						
晚	P: M:							
	晚	晚						
哪	P: M:							
	哪	哪						
儿	P: M:							
	儿	儿						
前	P: M:							
	前	前						
面	P: M:							
	面	面						

	P: M:							
后	后 后							

	P: M:							
右	右 右							

	P: M:							
边	边 边							

	P: M:							
左	左 左							

	P: M:							
里	里 里							

	P: M:							
外	外 外							

	P: M:							
回	回 回							

	P: M:							
来	来 来							

	P: M:							
怎	怎 怎							

4

事	P: M:								
见	事	事							
	P: M:								
穿	见	见							
	P: M:								
衣	穿	穿							
	P: M:								
服	衣	衣							
	P: M:								
先	服	服							
	P: M:								
太	先	先							
	P: M:								
黑	太	太							
	P: M:								
白	黑	黑							
	P: M:								
	白	白							

红	P: M:							
	红 红							
黄	P: M:							
	黄 黄							
蓝	P: M:							
	蓝 蓝							
绿	P: M:							
	绿 绿							
色	P: M:							
	色 色							
件	P: M:							
	件 件							
呢	P: M:							
	呢 呢							
找	P: M:							
	找 找							
多	P: M:							
	多 多							

5

九十八

少	P: M:									
	少	少								
钱	P: M:									
	钱	钱								
买	P: M:									
	买	买								
卖	P: M:									
	卖	卖								
块	P: M:									
	块	块								
毛	P: M:									
	毛	毛								
到	P: M:									
	到	到								
样	P: M:									
	样	样								
还	P: M:									
	还	还								

6

	P: M:								
要	要 要								
给	给 给								
谢	谢 谢								
本	本 本								
共	共 共								
空	空 空								
玩	玩 玩								
住	住 住								
电	电 电								

	P: M:								
话	话	话							

	P: M:								
请	请	请							

	P: M:								
问	问	问							

	P: M:								
进	进	进							

	P: M:								
等	等	等							

	P: M:								
出	出	出							

	P: M:								
时	时	时							

	P: M:								
间	间	间							

	P: M:								
该	该	该							

7

走

	走	走							

P:
M:

再

	再	再							

P:
M:

伟

	伟	伟							

P:
M:

兰

	兰	兰							

P:
M:

起

	起	起							

P:
M:

您

	您	您							

P:
M:

李

	李	李							

P:
M:

位

	位	位							

P:
M:

叔

	叔	叔							

一〇二

候	P: M:								
	候	候							
游	P: M:								
	游	游							
泳	P: M:								
	泳	泳							
城	P: M:								
	城	城							
双	P: M:								
	双	双							
功	P: M:								
	功	功							
夫	P: M:								
	夫	夫							
鞋	P: M:								
	鞋	鞋							
因	P: M:								
	因	因							

8

为	P: M:							
	为 为							
所	P: M:							
	所 所							
常	P: M:							
	常 常							
馆	P: M:							
	馆 馆							
子	P: M:							
	子 子							
饮	P: M:							
	饮 饮							
茶	P: M:							
	茶 茶							
都	P: M:							
	都 都							
平	P: M:							
	平 平							

一〇四

9

	P: M:									
客		客	客							
气	P: M:									
		气	气							
米	P: M:									
		米	米							
炒	P: M:									
		炒	炒							
得	P: M:									
		得	得							
雨	P: M:									
		雨	雨							
雪	P: M:									
		雪	雪							
刮	P: M:									
		刮	刮							
风	P: M:									
		风	风							

热

热 热

冷

冷 冷

凉

凉 凉

春

春 春

夏

夏 夏

秋

秋 秋

冬

冬 冬

北

北 北

京

京 京

P:
M:

一〇六

暖	P: M:								
	暖	暖							
阴	P: M:								
	阴	阴							
晴	P: M:								
	晴	晴							
最	P: M:								
	最	最							
高	P: M:								
	高	高							
低	P: M:								
	低	低							
度	P: M:								
	度	度							
	P: M:								
	P: M:								

| | P:
M: | | | | | | | | | |
| | | | | | | | | | | |

| | P:
M: | | | | | | | | | |
| | | | | | | | | | | |

| | P:
M: | | | | | | | | | |
| | | | | | | | | | | |

| | P:
M: | | | | | | | | | |
| | | | | | | | | | | |

| | P:
M: | | | | | | | | | |
| | | | | | | | | | | |

| | P:
M: | | | | | | | | | |
| | | | | | | | | | | |

| | P:
M: | | | | | | | | | |
| | | | | | | | | | | |

| | P:
M: | | | | | | | | | |
| | | | | | | | | | | |

| | P:
M: | | | | | | | | | |
| | | | | | | | | | | |

一〇八

This page is for you to play bingo or noughts & crosses.

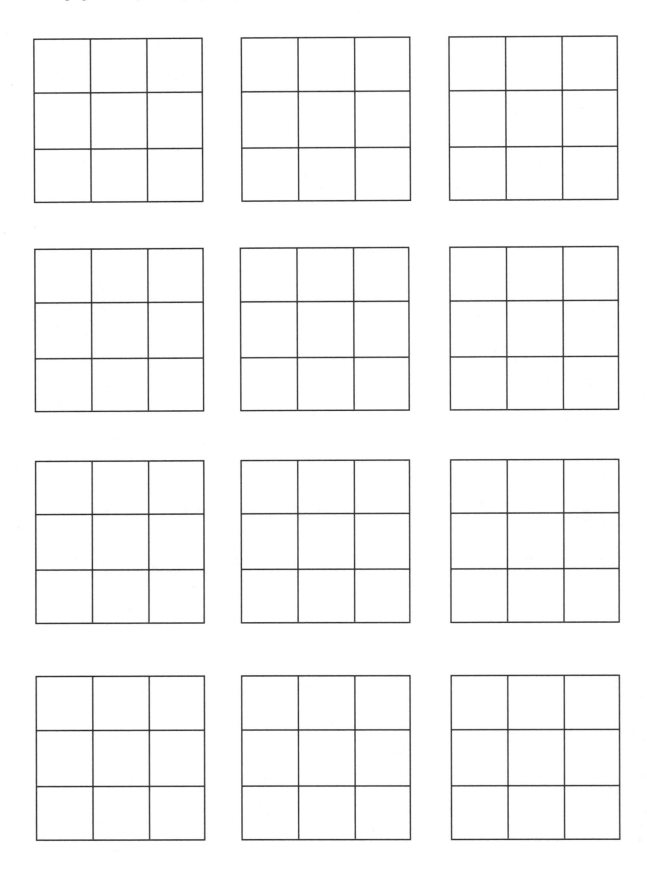